Money-Talks

Book 1.
How To Make Friends with Money

Book 2.
How To Create Savings

Book 3.
How To Cope with Credit Cards

Book 4.
How To Free Yourself from Debt

MONEY-TALKS

BOOK 4, SERIES 1

How To FREE YOURSELF FROM DEBT

JERROLD MUNDIS

Health Communications, Inc.
Deerfield Beach, Florida

ISBN 1-55874-274-3

Publisher: Health Communications, Inc.
3201 S.W. 15th Street
Deerfield Beach, FL 33442-8190

Cover design by Robert Cannata

How To Free Yourself From Debt

Part I: The Concepts

Part II: The Techniques

Introduction

How To Free Yourself From Debt

You don't have to be in debt. Regardless of how long you've been there, how much you owe or even how much you make. No one does, no matter what you might have thought up to now. You can free yourself from debt and stay free — forever.

Money-Talks is a series of booklets that have been created to help you gain a happier and more prosperous relationship with your money — to enable you to manage it more effectively, bring more of it in and use it in more pleasurable ways.

They accomplish this in two ways: First, by providing you with new *Concepts* about money that will change your thinking and open up new possibilities of emotion and action for you. Second, by giving you specific *Techniques* to use that will bring about immediate positive results.

At the end of each booklet there is also a "Resource Library," a list of books that will help you explore the topic further.

Now let's learn how to free yourself from debt.

User's Guide

This user's guide is designed to help you gain the maximum benefit from *How to Free Yourself from Debt*. The best way to work with the book is to follow the three guidelines below:

First, read through it once, slowly. (Return to it later as often as you wish.)

Second, meditate and reflect upon the concepts. Make them an integral part of your consciousness.

Third, practice the techniques on a regular basis.

The more you meditate on the concepts and practice the techniques, the more successful you will be in freeing yourself from debt — and in gaining a happier and more prosperous relationship with money.

Also, take advantage of the Resource Library. The books there will provide you with additional tools that can enrich and expand the process of freeing yourself from debt.

PART I

The Concepts

Beginning

Most of our problems with debt stem from negative attitudes and perceptions about money and about ourselves in relationship to it. For example: "I don't deserve much." Or "No one can get ahead in this kind of economy." Many of these lie just below the surface of our minds. We don't think about them much, but they're there anyway, ruling our emotions and actions with the power of a dictator.

This section contains new, *real* and constructive attitudes and perceptions about money and about yourself in relationship to it. Understanding them, and making them a part of your thinking, is the first step in freeing yourself from debt.

1. What Is Debt?

What is debt?

In its simpliest definition, you are in debt when you owe some person or institution money. We need a refinement though. For our purposes, a secured loan is *not* a debt, even though money has been loaned to you.

To secure something is to make it safe. Security, or collateral, is property you pledge to the lender or actually give to him to hold during the course of the loan. When you pay him back he returns it to you. A loan from a pawnshop is a classic example. Another form is a mortgage; here, your house secures the loan.

Why Secured Loans Are Not Debt

From a strict point of view, a secured loan *is* debt: It's money you "owe." But there is a difference, and that difference is crucial. If things go wrong, for any reason at all, and you can't repay the loan, what happens? You forfeit your property. That may be painful, but you *are not obligated to pay money to anyone.*

You walk away clean. you don't owe anyone money. You're not in debt.

This Is It

So debt is:

1. Any amount of cash you borrow without putting up collateral. (Tapping a friend at the office for $20.)
2. Any credit extended to you. (Charging a new lawn mower to your Sears account.)
3. Any service you take without paying for it at the moment you receive it. (Arranging to pay your dentist

off over the next several months.)

and

4. Falling behind on unsecured obligations. (Not paying your rent in the month that it's due.)

2. A Supermarket Of Opportunities

Supermarkets, in the main, are a welcome convenience: They offer abundance, variety, and require little effort. Unfortunately, the same is true of our daily lives when it comes to debt:

"Fly now, pay later."

"Take advantage of new low interest rates."

"Only twelve low monthly payments."

"Your preapproved credit line."

"Accepted everywhere."

"Time-option payment plan."
"Just sign and return this agreement today."
"Call our toll-free operator."
"Send no money now."
"No membership fee."

We borrow from banks and financial institutions, employers, merchants, and the government; colleges and universities, business associates, acquaintances, co-workers, friends and relatives. We borrow for downpayments on houses, when we're between jobs, for education, vacations, Christmas buying, for furniture, medical expenses, big tax bills, births, marriages, divorces, to get over a hump or when things are difficult in general.

There is a great supermarket of oppotunities out there. And not only is the door wide open, but someone is waving us through at every moment: Pick a debt, any debt.

3. A Form Of Poverty

Debt is a form of poverty. A particularly cruel one: It makes you *think* you have more money than you do.

Using credit — which is simply going into debt — does not give you more money. Or more freedom, power or bounty. It actually gives you less.

It gives you the *illusion* of more.

4. The Best Investment Of All

If you were offered a choice between paying off your unsecured debt and putting the same amount of money into any investment you wanted, you'd come out far ahead by choosing to pay off your debt.

The practical effect of paying off credit-card or other high-interest debt is the same as investing that money at 16 to 24 percent. By contrast, money market funds, at this writing, are paying about 2½ percent.

If you invested $3,000 at 2½ percent and let it sit for nine years you would have $4,000. If you invested $3,000 at 24 percent and let it sit for nine years you would have $21,000.

Paying off your unsecured debt offers you something no other investment can: a rate of return that is *high, risk-free and guaranteed.* It's the best investment you can make.

5. Whose Money Are We Talking About?

Your creditors don't want your money. They want *their* money.

The bank, the telephone company, the little shop around the corner and your sister don't want a single penny of yours. All they want is the money they loaned you.

They gave you cash or merchandise or services because you asked them to and because you told them you'd return the money or pay for what you received.

So when a creditor asks you to

do that, he's not asking for your money — he's asking for his money, and only under the terms of the deal you made with him.

Remember whose money we're talking about.

6. Bankruptcy and Home Equity Loans: Nyet! (The Money Comes In)

Bankruptcy is a bad idea for most people with a debt problem. It does nothing to alter the beliefs and behavior that underlie a problem with debt, it often leads to a sense of shame and failure which only intensifies the debting syndrome and it plagues your credit record for ten years. Further, it encourages you to think that if things get tough, you can always go that route again, thus destroying your opportunity to truly liberate yourself from debt and live free of it forever. Sooner or later — usually sooner — most people with a debt problem who declare bankruptcy end up in the same kind of trouble again.

Home equity loans aren't much more desirable. Thousands of people have lost their homes through eventually becoming unable to make the payments on these loans. Many more have squandered the only asset they ever had — the equity in their house.

While bankruptcy or a home-equity loan may in a rare case be useful in freeing oneself from debt, that is true only when they are used as a part of a larger recovery program. They are never a solution in themselves.

When you're committed to freeing yourself from debt, and you absorb the concepts and practice the techniques in this book, there is always enough; the money comes in.

That doesn't mean that you always get what you want or when you want it or in the form that you want it. But in the end, the money comes in. There is always enough.

PART II

The Techniques

Continuing

Integrating the concepts into your daily thinking is important and will go a long way toward helping you free yourself from debt. But the concepts themselves aren't enough.

The second part of the process is to take action, to practice certain techniques. This is something like saying, "Faith without works is dead." You need the concepts, but you have to practice the techniques too.

Each will make the other more effective and easier to work with.

This section contains twelve powerful techniques that will help you free yourself from debt.

1. One Day

Here is something you can do immediately.

Just for today, one day, do not incur any new debt.

- Don't borrow $2 from a friend.
- Don't accept a service you plan to pay for later.
- Don't take a loan from a bank.
- Don't charge anything on your credit card.

Just go through today, this one small 24-hour period, without taking on any new debt in any form. Resolve to do that. Then close this book and spend the rest of the day enjoying yourself.

Do it now . . .

2. One Day At A Time

Congratulations! You didn't go one penny further into debt yesterday. You proved that it's possible not to incur a new debt for one day. You have just accomplished the single most important part of the program.

This is the threshold:

Just for today, you're not going to incur any new debt.

We're only talking about one day — today. Tomorrow is irrelevant. What you might to do tomorrow, next week, next month, next year doesn't matter. They're not here yet. All that is real, ever, is today. And today, one day at a time, you're not going to incur any new debt.

Anyone can avoid debt for a single day.

Here is a simple but profound truth:

You cannot get out of debt by borrowing more money.

No more than an alcoholic can become sober by having another drink.

Tomorrow is irrelevant: It's one day at a time. And just for today, for one day, you don't debt.

3. The Plastic, Of Course

You probably feared this was coming. Indeed it was, and here it is: Keeping a credit card in your wallet is like carrying around a hand grenade with a loose pin — sooner or later it's going to go off.

There is only one thing you can do with a credit card: debt. That's a simple fact, yet few are willing to face it at first, even among people who have clearly brutalized themselves with credit cards. It's true that without credit cards you'll sometimes have to think a bit, make alternate arrangements and now and then be inconvenienced. But the benefits you'll gain from getting rid of the cards far outweigh the few difficulties you'll encounter.

Therefore . . .

Right — take all your plastic and cut it up. If you don't have the cards, you can't use them. Notify the supplier that you wish to cancel the account. Most will try to talk you out of that, which is natural since they make a tremendous profit on the cards. Be friendly and polite, but remain firm.

4. An Exception

Some people feel they *need* a credit card. Business people who travel frequently, for example. A card simplifies their many necessary transactions and helps them keep records. If you are rock sure of your personal discipline, and have an unequivocal need for a credit card, then do this:

1. Retain only one card.
2. Carry the card only on business days.
3. Write out a check in the amount you charged on the same day, then deduct that

amount from your balance.

This last is essential — and consistent with the principle and practice of not debting. You spent that money today, it is no longer available to you.

In place of a credit card you might wish to carry a debit or secured card, or a company card with charges billable directly to your employer. All of these can give you the advantages of a credit card without the liabilities.

5. The Three-Month Overview

Keep a record of every expenditure you make for three months — from a 25¢ pack of gum to a $75 sweater. At the end of every week total up your expenses, in categories such as car, clothes, groceries, home furnishings and the like, and enter them onto a one-month record.

Use a form something like the simplified one on the next page.

SPENDING RECORD FOR MARCH

Week	1	2	3	4	Total
Car					
Clothes					
Entertainment					
Gas & Electricity					
Groceries					
Medical					
Papers & Magazines					
Rent					
Telephone					
Totals:					

Break your spending into twenty-five to thirty-five categories: too few, you're still foggy; too many, you overcomplicate the record.

Keeping this record will help you to see clearly — perhaps for the first time — where your money is really going, which is an important step in taking control of your money.

6. The Plan

The Spending Plan is designed to help you match your income to expenses. It is *not* a budget. It is merely a set of guidelines to point you in the direction you wish to go. Create a Spending Plan by expanding on the form you're using for your Spending Record. Alter that form in this fashion:

1. Change the name of the last vertical column on the right from "Total to "Actual."
2. Add a new vertical column to the right of that one,

named "Plan."

3. Add a final vertical column to the right of the "Plan" column and mark this one "+" Or "–", which indicates plus or minus.

On the next page is a simple example.

SPENDING PLAN FOR APRIL

Week	1	2	3	4	Actual	Plan	+Or–
Car							
Clothes							
Entertainment							
Gas & Electricity							
Groceries							
Medical							
Papers & Magazines							
Rent							
Telephone							
Totals:							

How to Use It

Get out last month's Spending Record. Think about what you spent, one category at a time. Does it seem you spent too much here, or maybe not enough? Pick a reasonable figure, given your income and other expenses, and enter it in the "Plan" column. Go through each of your categories this way.

At the end of the month use the last three columns to measure how well you did and to help you formulate your plan for the coming month.

7. Two Basic Ways

There are two basic ways to avoid debt in the early stages: cut expenses or bring in more money. Most people use a combination. The list below is meant to provide you with some practical ideas, but more to fire your own imagination. Keep in mind that most of these early measures are only temporary. As you progress you'll be operating with steadily increasing income.

- Review the necessity of each expenditure. If you don't absolutely need to make it, defer it.

- Cash a check or take money out of your savings account, even if it's the last money in there.
- Brown bag your lunch to work instead of buying it out.
- Empty the container into which you toss your loose change. For most people, this gives them an immediate $20 to $200.
- Liquidate an asset, such as a stock certificate or bond, even if you take a loss on it.
- Exchange services — clerical work in your doctor's office

for the services you need from him. Trade your expertise in any area for someone else's that you need.

- Collect a debt owed to you, money you loaned to someone.
- Inform a client you can't front the cost of materials and bill him later; he must pay for the materials at the start.
- Cancel an order and reclaim your deposit.
- Request a small cash gift from a relative.
- Ask your employer to give

you the commission already owed to you for sales already made.

- Stay home and watch television instead of going out to a movie.

Write out your own list. Let your imagination run free. Be as wild and improbable as you can. Hurdle old mental barricades, break out into the open. Some of your ideas will be more desirable than others, and not all will be feasible. That's fine — the point is to get down as many as possible.

8. The Proportional Paydown

It's time to add a new category to your Spending Plan — Debt Repayment. The amount is irrelevant. Payments nearly always start small. In fact, some people make none at all for several months. It is necessary to stablize first, to make sure that expenses do not exceed income.

"But that's impossible! My creditors won't wait, and they'd never accept $5 a month!"

Yes they will, if you're being honest. They have little choice.

They may not like it, they may insult you, threaten you and even take agressive action. But you will prevail. Even in court, if it goes that far. Which it usually doesn't. So long as you remain honest and stick to your purpose no one can force you to pay them more than you can actually afford to pay.

Get out your Spending Plan. Place a calculator, a pad and a pencil at hand.

Now:

1. Consult your Spending Plan. Determine how much — in

total — you could reasonably pay toward your debts each month without harming yourself. Let's say, for purposes of illustration below, that the amount is $50.

2. Make a list of all your creditors and the amount you owe each one.
3. Add up your total debt.
4. Use your calculator to determine each creditor's share, or percentage, of the total. The formula is: Creditor's Amount ÷ Total Debt = Creditor's Percentage.

For Example:

You owe your sister $750. Your total debt is $6400. Divide the amount you owe your sister ($750) by your total debt ($6400). The anwser equals your sister's share — or percentage — of your total debt.

Sister		Total Debt		Sister's Share
$750	÷	$6400	=	.12 or 12%

Do this for each of your creditors. The result might look like this:

Total Debt: $6400

Creditor			Total		Share
Chase Bank ..	$4250	÷	$6400	=	66%
MasterCard	900	÷	6400	=	14
Sister	750	÷	6400	=	12
Bob	500	÷	6400	=	8
	$6400		100%		

5. Now multiply each creditor's percentage by the total amount you can pay each month. To illustrate:

Sister's Share		Total Payment		Sister's Payment
12%	x	$50	=	$6.00

Follow this procedure for each of your creditors. For example:

Total Money Available Each Month For Repayment: $50

Creditor's Share			Total Pymt.		Share
Chase Bank ...	66%	x	$50	=	$33.00
MasterCard ...	14	x	50	=	7.00
Sister	12	x	50	=	6.00
Bob	8	x	50	=	4.00
	100%				$50.00

"But those are chickenfeed numbers! I'm $75,000 in debt!"

Some people owe more than

you do, some less. The numbers don't matter: The principle remains the same.

"It'll take forever to pay off $6400 at $50 a month!"

It only seems that way. Payments nearly always start small. They increase as time passes. The process builds on itself; in the end repayment is often rapid and dramatic.

What matters is that you have completely reversed your situation. You are now getting *out* of debt instead of *into* debt. That is a stunning achievement.

9. Negotiating

Take the initiative with your creditors: Get in touch with them rather than waiting for them to come to you. Set up an appointment if you can. A personal meeting is always the most effective way to deal with a creditor. If that's not possible, use the telephone. If you can't get through by phone, write a letter. But whichever, take the initiative.

Be prepared. Have all the facts and figures at hand.

Explain your situation forthrightly.

Tell your creditor that you regret this situation, that you are determined to correct it and that you are committed to repaying him in full.

Negotiate according to the realities of your spending and repayment plans. Remember, they are real. You cannot repay more than you are capable of repaying; and you know what that figure is.

If you wish, tell your creditor you have undertaken a financial recovery program.

Remain calm through all your dealings with your creditor — regardless of his behavior. If you don't feel calm, act so anyway. Reacting out of anger or fear will only work to your detriment.

Remember that you are not in an inferior position when you negotiate with a creditor, regardless of any emotions you might have to the contrary. You are one of two parties in a simple business transaction. You both want the same thing: for the money to be repaid. All that's under discussion is the best way to do that. You know clearly what's possible for you, and what isn't. Your job is to convey that information to your creditor.

10. Moratoriums And Restructuring

Some creditors will grant you a moratorium — a temporary suspension of payments — for three to six months if you truly need one and explain your problem clearly. Moratoriums are usually granted only on the principal; you continue to pay the interest or finance charges.

Other creditors may be willing to restructure a loan — extend the time period over which it is to be repaid, which reduces the amount due each month.

Write out a loose script for yourself before you approach the creditor so you're confident you have all the appropriate information and know what you're going to say.

11. Bye-bye

With gratitude, kiss your enablers goodbye.

An enabler is someone who makes it easier for you to keep debting — usually a relative or friend, sometimes a business associate. Most often an enabler is well meaning. He cares about you. He wants to help you out of a tight spot.

Sometimes there's a darker side to enablers: Consciously or subconsciously they may be motivated by a desire to keep you dependent or under their control.

Regardless of the enabler's motivation — even if it's purely loving and selfless — his act of enabling only damages you, only makes it easier for you to continue to debt.

So thank your enablers for their concern and desire to help. Tell them you're grateful for the help they've already given you and that the best way you can demonstrate your gratitude is to pay them back in full as soon as you can; and that that day will come much sooner if you don't borrow any more from them.

Then, kiss them goodbye.

12. Congratulations

Congratulations. From me and the countless thousands of others just like you who have already freed themselves from debt or who are freeing themselves right now.

This is a brave and wonderful thing you are doing. It's not always easy. In fact, sometimes it can be downright scary, even painful. But the scope of the freedom you will gain, and the confidence and self-esteem, are extraordinary: far beyond anything you can imagine at the moment.

Freeing yourself from debt is one of the very best things you can do — *in* your life and *for* your life.

Godspeed.

A Closing Note

Freeing yourself from debt is a living process. This little book won't do you much good gathering dust in the corner of a shelf. Use it. Work with it. Integrate its material into your life on a daily basis. The more you do, the better off you'll be. If you practice its techniques and absorb its concepts you *will* free yourself from debt, you *will* remain free and you *will* go on to live prosperously, in a state of thriving, and to know abundance, to have all that you need in ample supply.

May you know happiness and pleasure as you do.

The Resource Library

All of these books will help you free yourself from debt. Some never mention debt or the word money at all, but may be more helpful than those focused entirely on those subjects. That depends on the needs of the individual reader.

Healers on Healing edited by Richard Carlson and Benjamin Shield. Jermy P. Tarcher, 1989.

Happiness Is an Inside Job by John Powell, S.J. Tabor Publishing, 1989.

How to Get Out of Debt, Stay Out of Debt & Live Prosperously by Jerrold Mundis. Bantam Books, 1988.

Money is my Friend by Phil Laut. Trinity Publications, 1978.

Money Troubles by Robin Leonard. Nolo Press, 1991.

The Richest Man in Babylon by George S. Clason. Bantam Books, 1985.

You Can Negotiate Anything by Herb Cohen. Lyle Stuart, 1980.

A Whack on the Side of the Head by Roger von Oech. Warner Books, revised edition, 1990.

When Money is The Drug by Donna Boundy. HarperSanFrancisco 1993.

Your Maximum Mind by Herbert Benson, M.D., with William Proctor. Times Books, 1987.

Two Additional Resources

You may also find one or both of the following organizations helpful:

Debtors Anonymous
General Service Board
Box 400
Grand Central Station
New York, NY 10163-0400

and:

The National Foundation for
Consumer Credit
8611 Second Avenue
Suite 100
Silver Spring, MD 20910
(Telephone: 301-589-5600)

Debtors Anonymous is self-help program with cha ters in many parts of th country. The National Foun dation for Consumer Credit a nonprofit institution wi branch offices in every state